Howard Skempton

Collected Piano Pieces

Many of the pieces in this volume, and pieces from Howard Skempton: *Images* are included on the Sony Classical compact disc, 'Howard Skempton: Well, well, Cornelius', SK66482, performed by John Tilbury.

Oxford University Press, Walton Street, Oxford OX2 6DP, England
Oxford University Press Inc., 198 Madison Avenue, New York, NY 10016, USA

for Donald and Kathleen

COLLECTED PIANO PIECES

First Prelude

HOWARD SKEMPTON

Printed in Great Britain
OXFORD UNIVERSITY PRESS, MUSIC DEPARTMENT, WALTON STREET, OXFORD OX2 6DP

September 1971

One for Molly

HOWARD SKEMPTON

Simple Piano Piece

HOWARD SKEMPTON

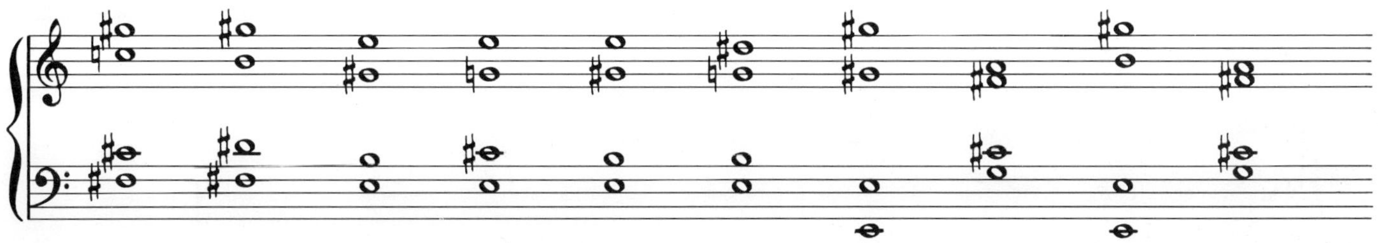

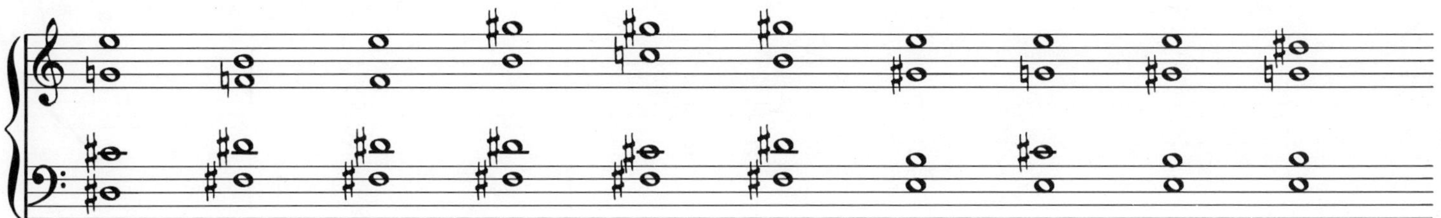

August 1972

Intermezzo

HOWARD SKEMPTON

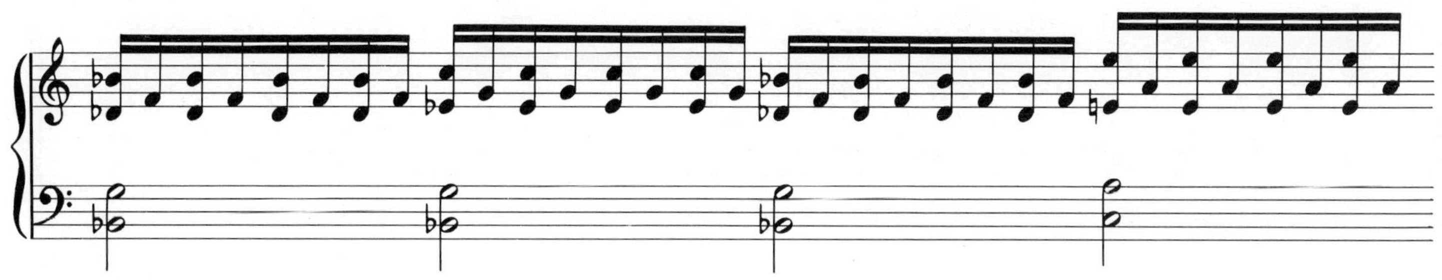

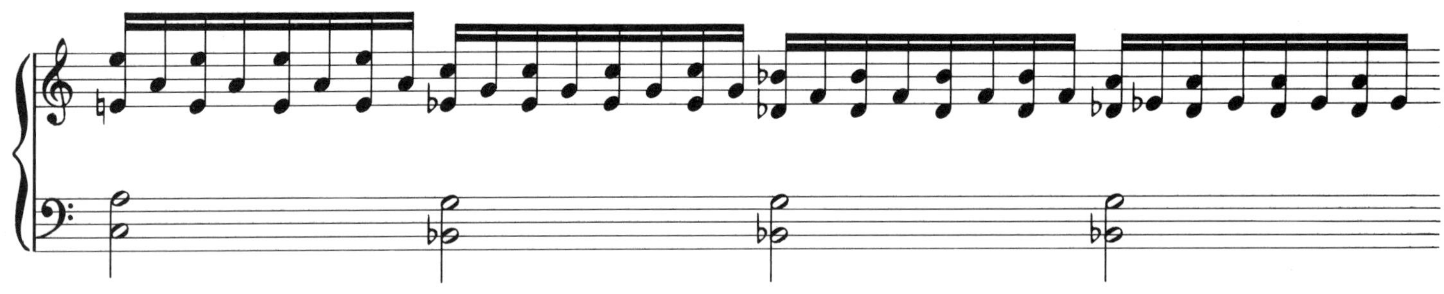

February 1973

Riding the Thermals

HOWARD SKEMPTON

June 1973

Slow Waltz

three hands

HOWARD SKEMPTON

July 1973

Quavers

HOWARD SKEMPTON

Slowly and very quietly

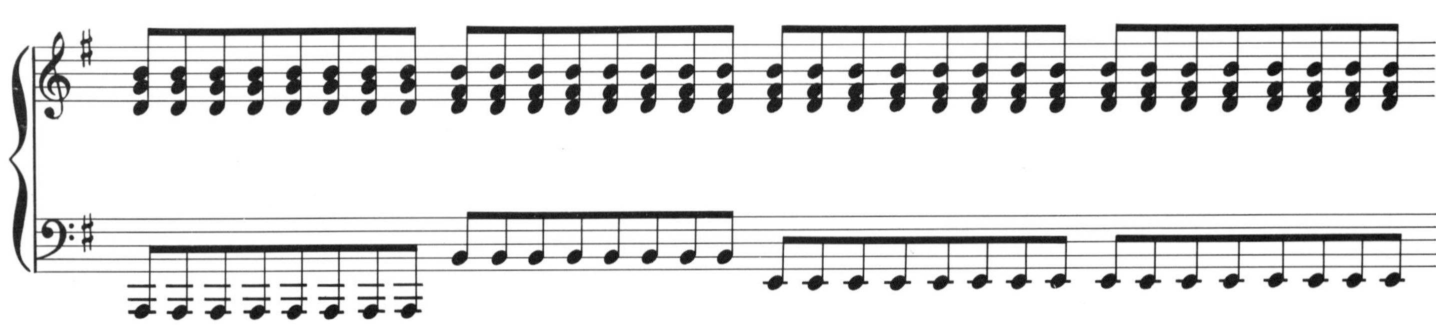

May 1972

A Humming Song

HOWARD SKEMPTON

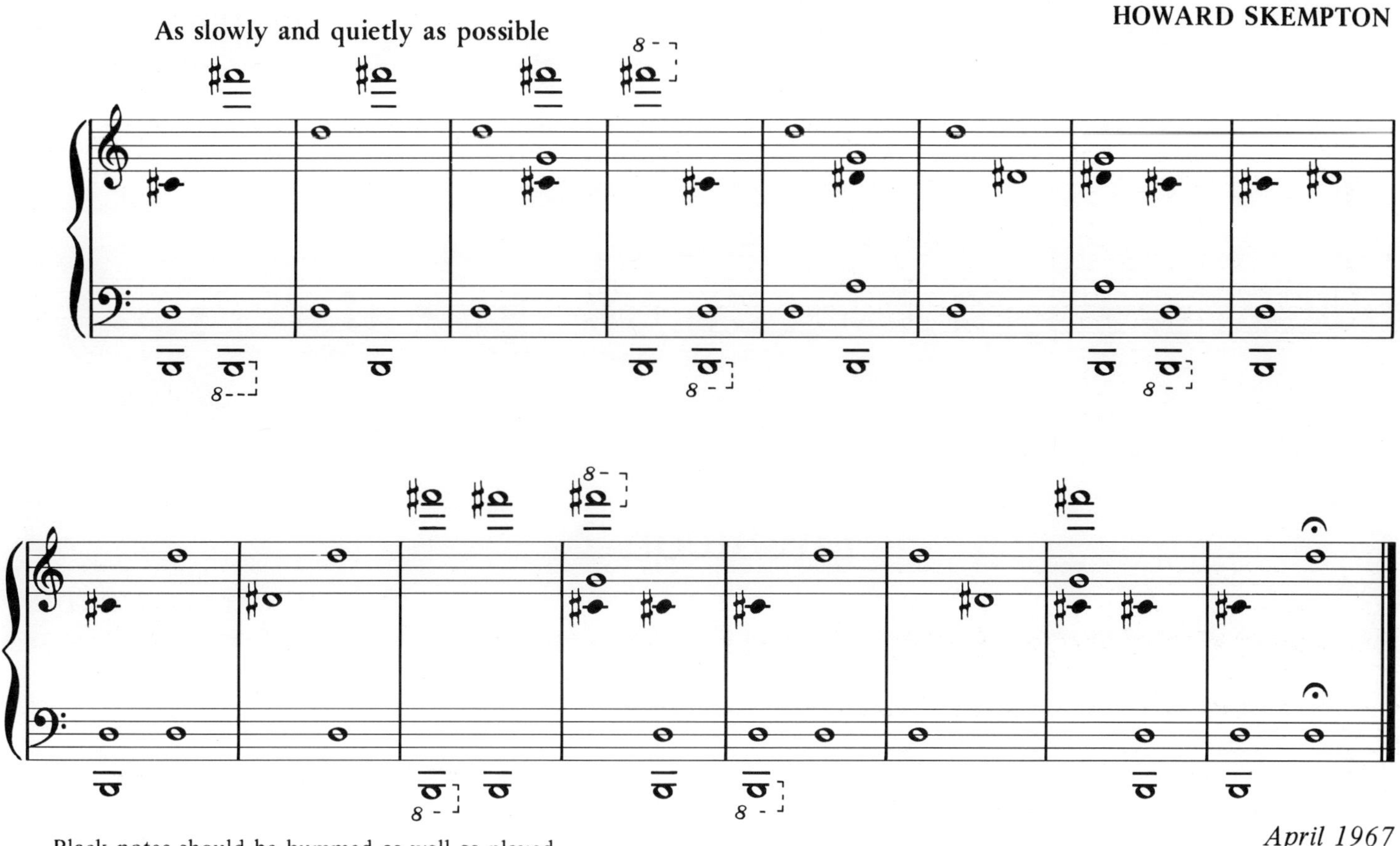

Black notes should be hummed as well as played.

April 1967

September Song

HOWARD SKEMPTON

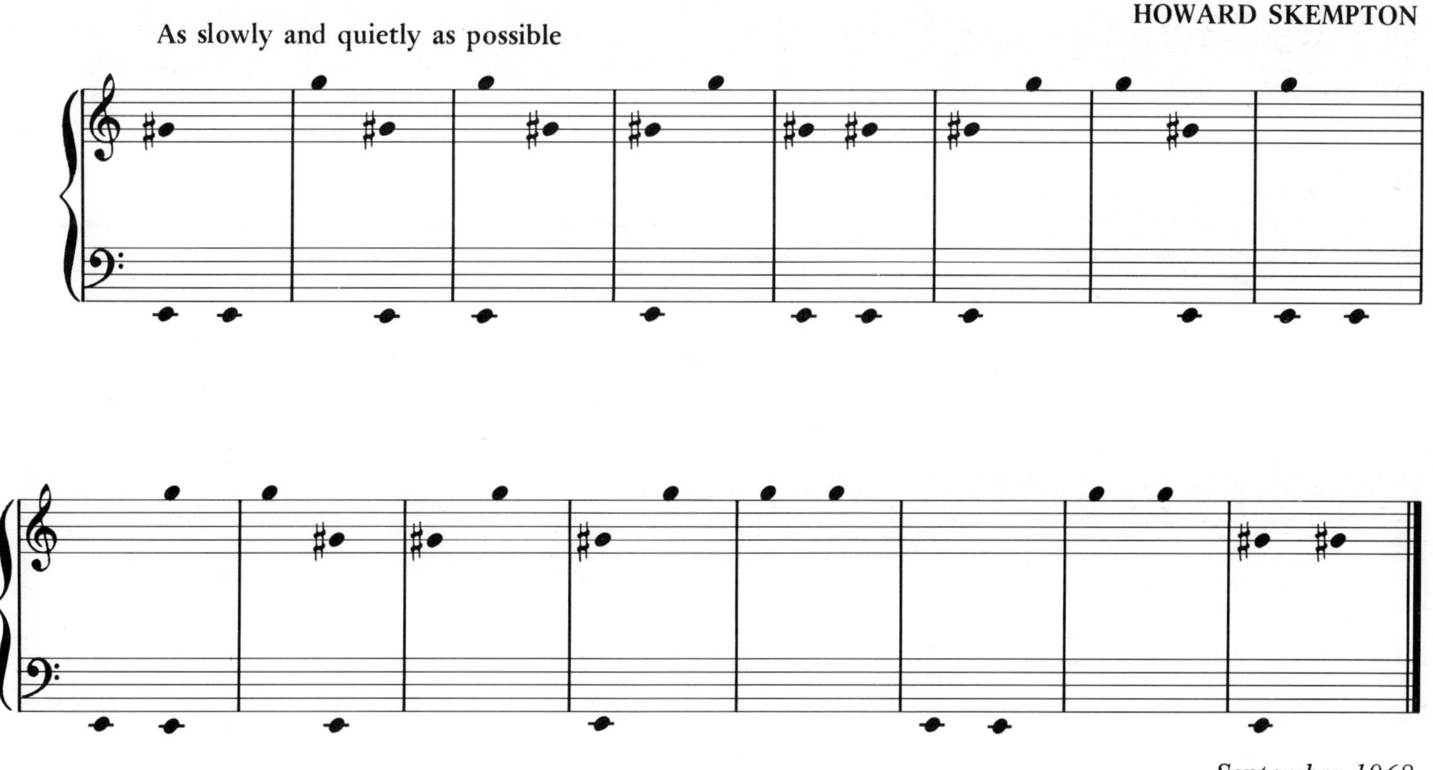

September 1968

for Andrew and Lotta

Eirenicon

HOWARD SKEMPTON

31 August 1973

Eirenicon 2

HOWARD SKEMPTON

August 1977

Eirenicon 3

HOWARD SKEMPTON

12 June 1978

for Michael Finnissy

Eirenicon 4

HOWARD SKEMPTON

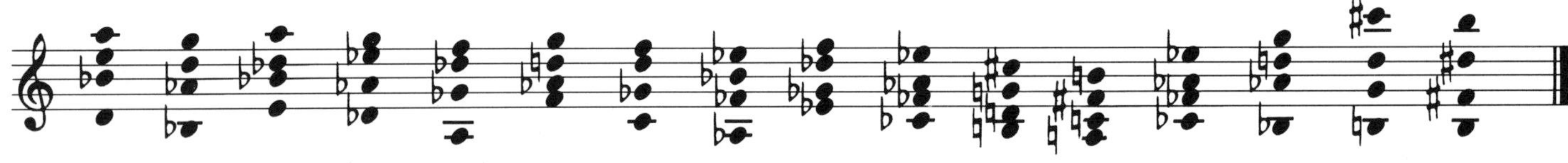

August 1985

to Michael Finnissy

Even Tenor

HOWARD SKEMPTON

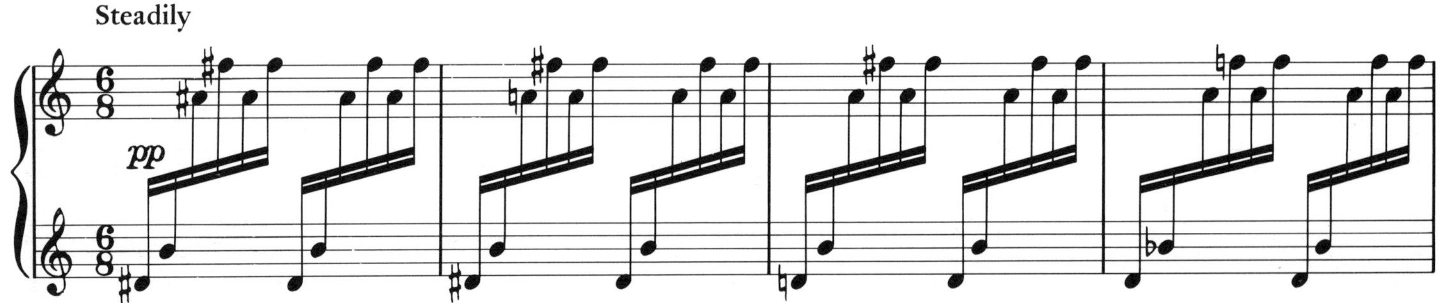

December 1988

Piano Piece 1969

HOWARD SKEMPTON

Very slowly and quietly

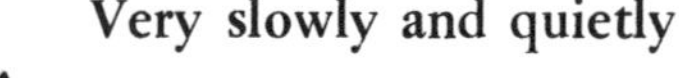

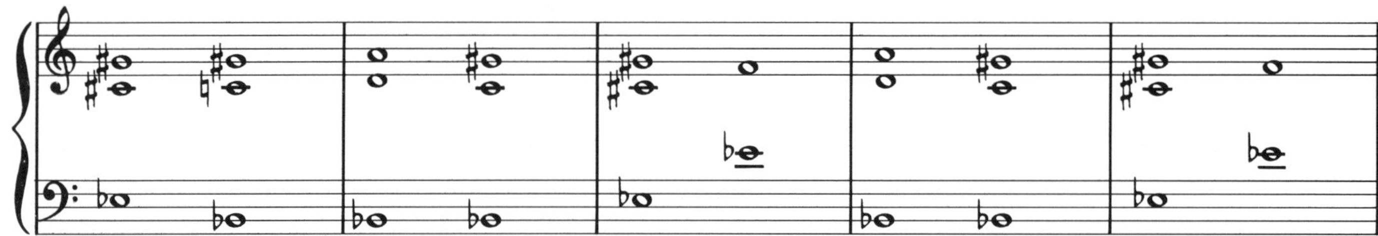

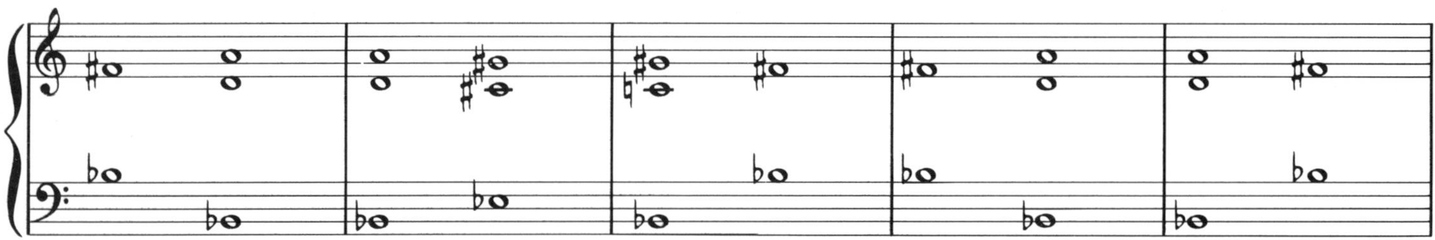

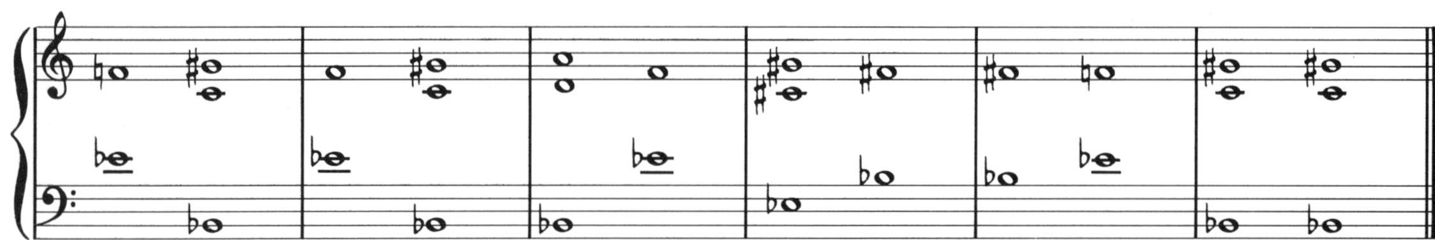

December 1969

for Peter Hill

Trace

for right hand

HOWARD SKEMPTON

Gently

27 August 1980

Air

HOWARD SKEMPTON

Moderato

p

28 August 1979

for Simon and Daniel

Saltaire Melody

HOWARD SKEMPTON

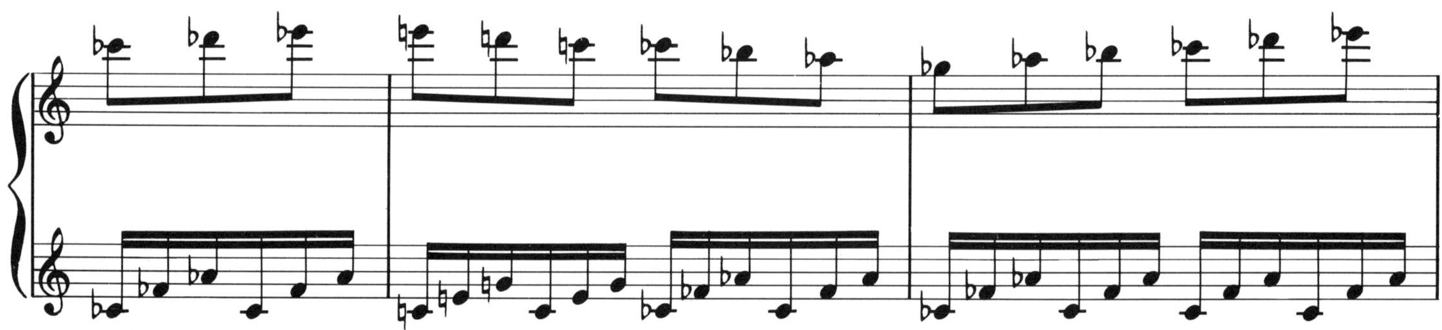

30 November 1977

for Benjamin Britten

senza licenza

for left hand

HOWARD SKEMPTON

Slowly and quietly

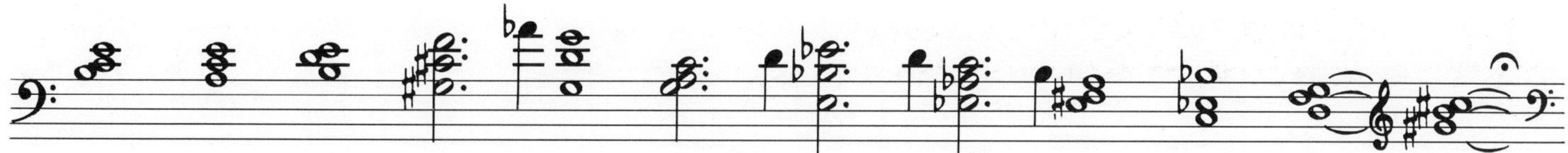

Accidentals apply only to the notes they immediately precede.

26 August 1974

for Benjamin Britten

Invention

for left hand

HOWARD SKEMPTON

Gently

13 November 1974

for Benjamin Britten

passing fancy

for left hand

HOWARD SKEMPTON

April 1975

for Benjamin Britten

Chorale

for left hand

HOWARD SKEMPTON

20 June 1976

Rumba

HOWARD SKEMPTON

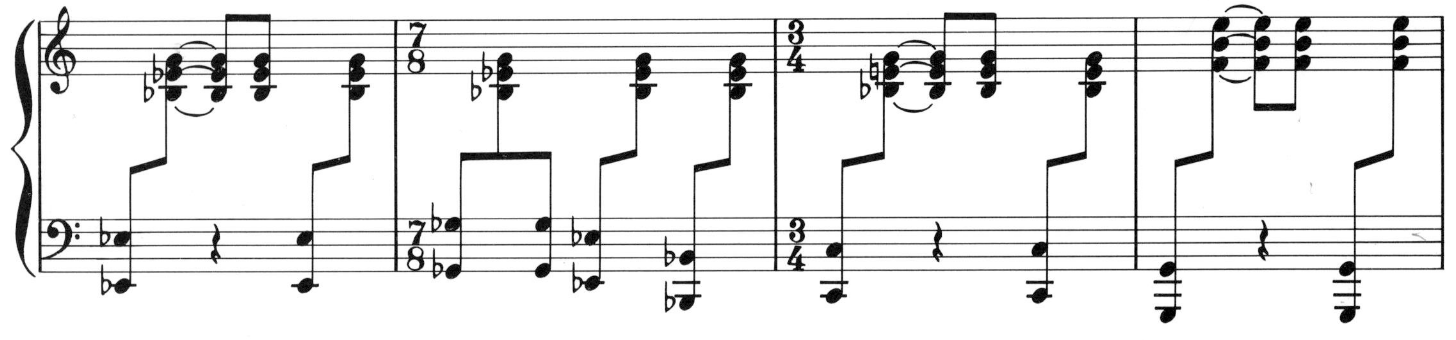

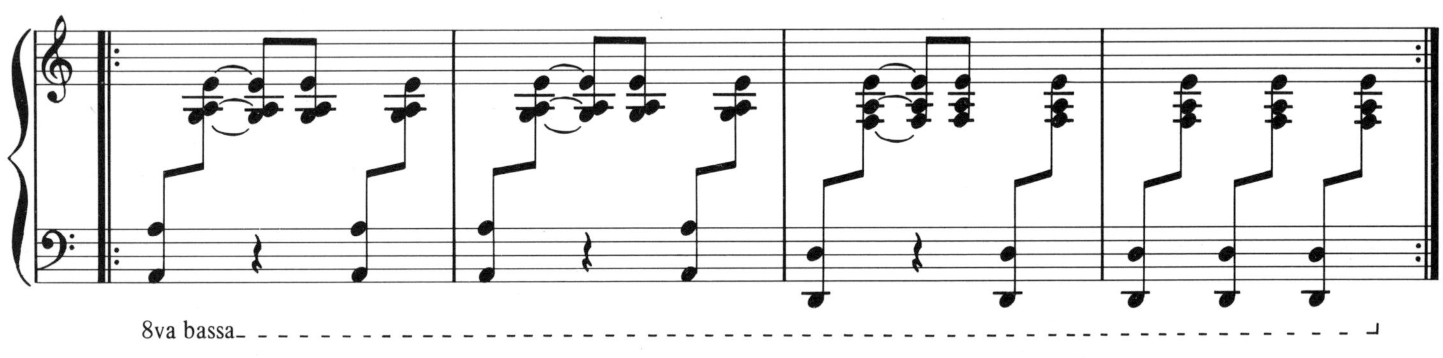
8va bassa

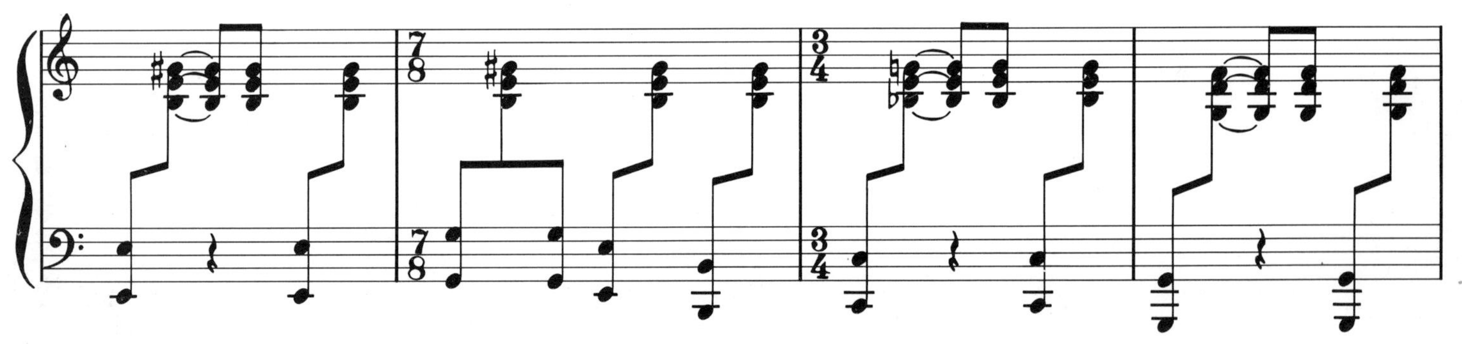

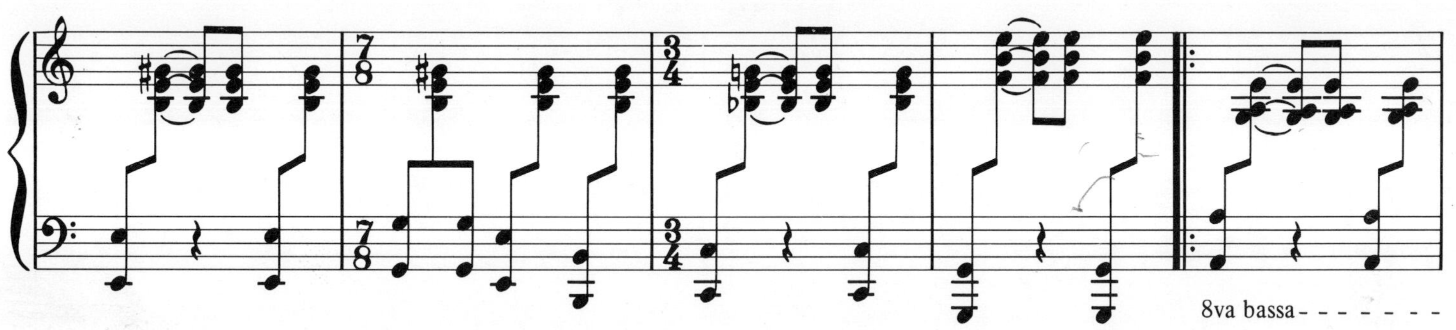

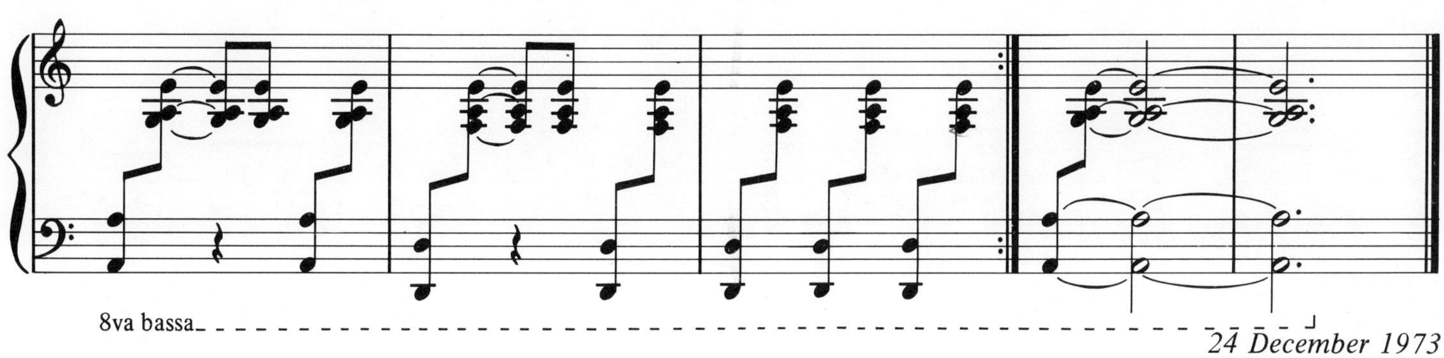

24 December 1973

in memory of Morton Feldman

Toccata

HOWARD SKEMPTON

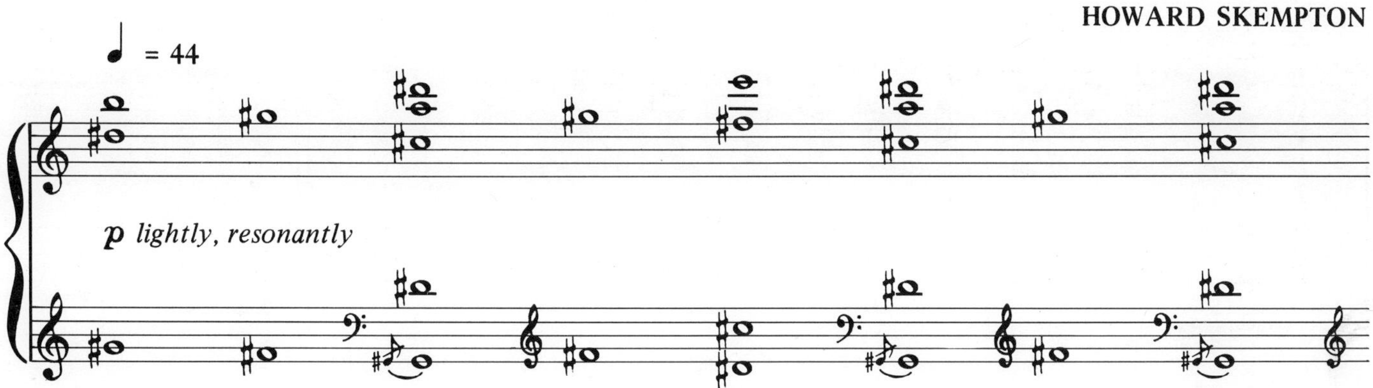

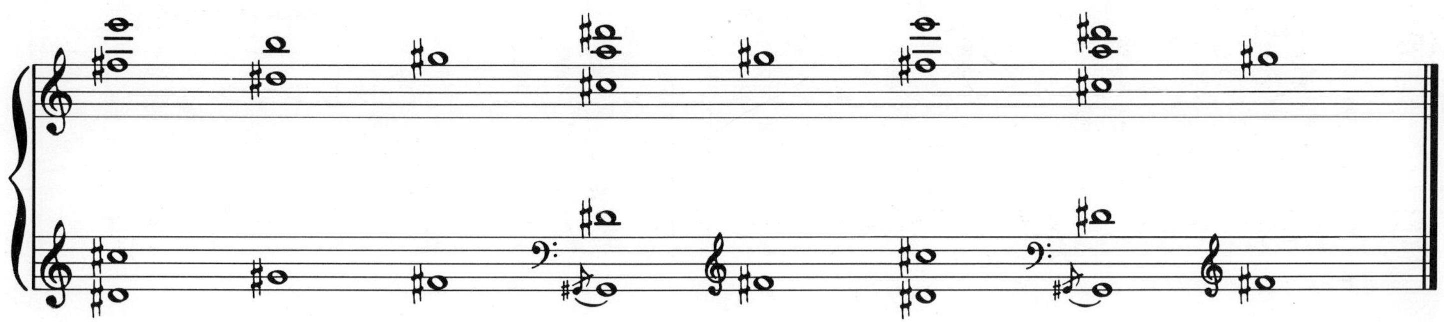

December 1987

for Colin Matthews

Quavers 5

HOWARD SKEMPTON

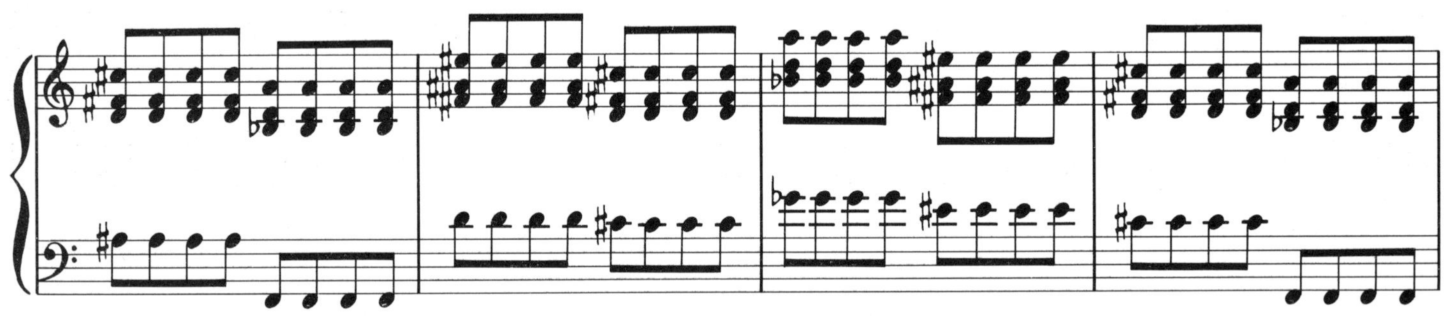

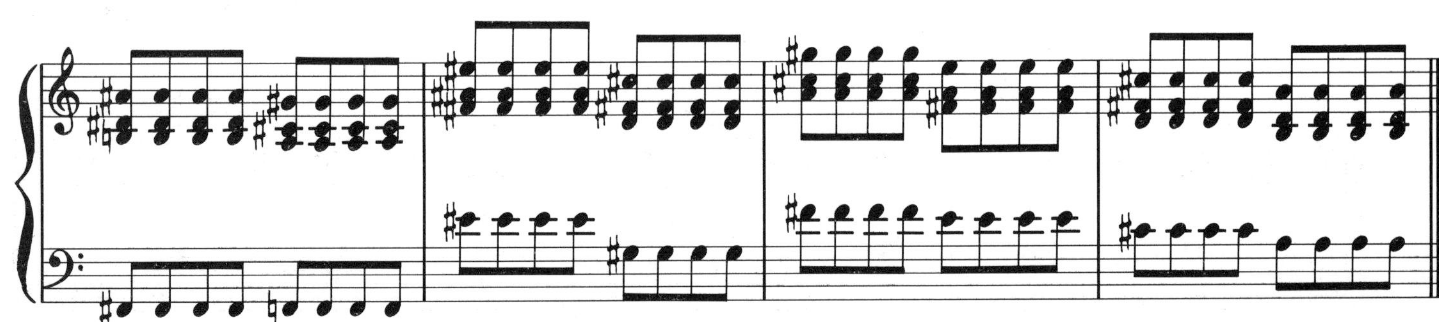

February 1984

for John Tilbury

A Roma

HOWARD SKEMPTON

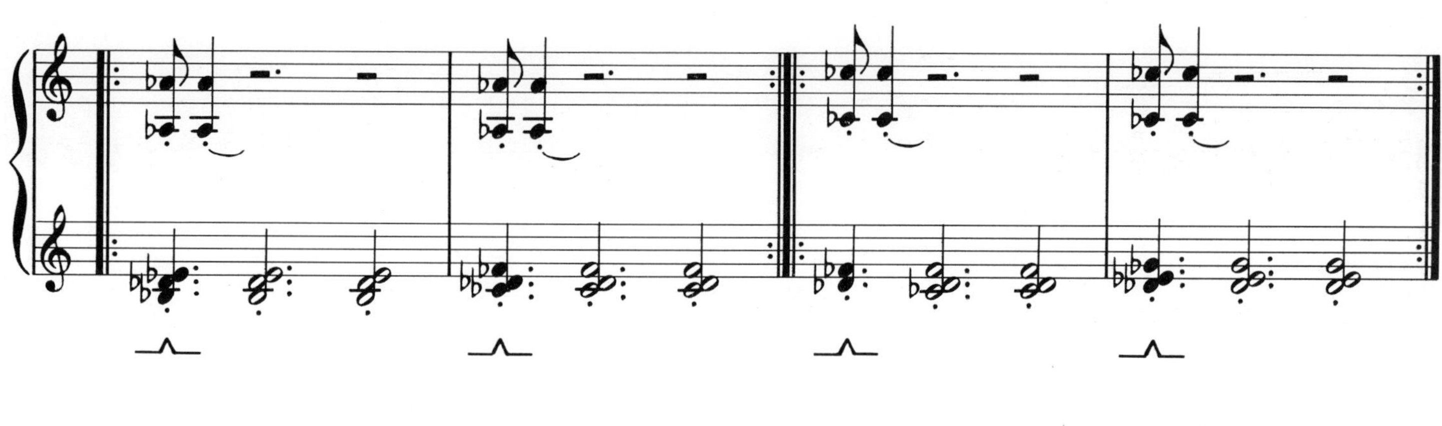

2 April 1992

in memory of John Cage

Of Late

HOWARD SKEMPTON

25 September 1992

Well, well, Cornelius

HOWARD SKEMPTON

(Well, well, Corne - lius, your life is end - ed, it's o - ver. But your
mp
work goes on as be - fore.)
mf
rall.
f

June 1982

June '77

HOWARD SKEMPTON

June 1977

for Giancarlo

Campanella 3

HOWARD SKEMPTON

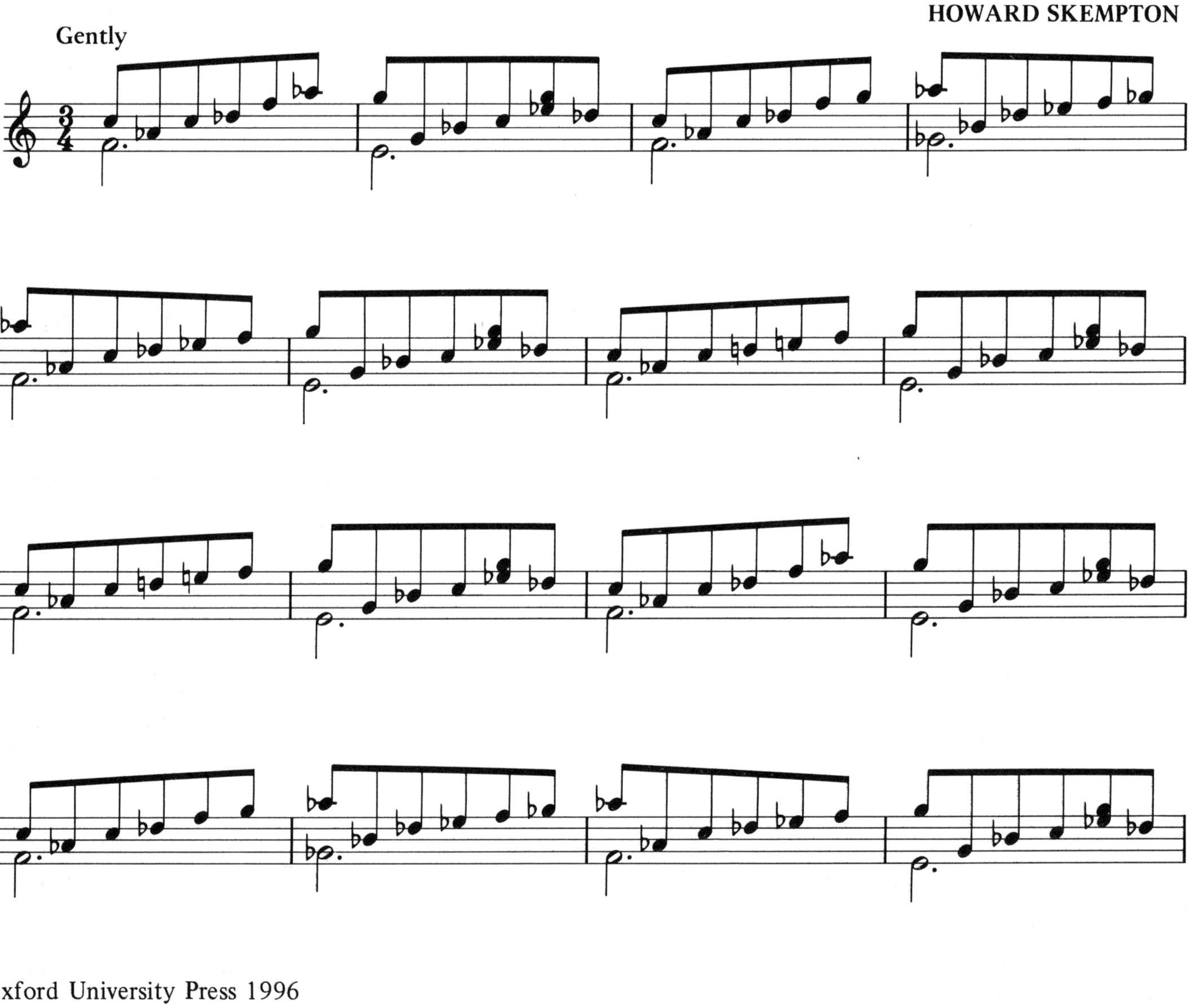

Gently

October 1982

to Giancarlo Cardini

Campanella

HOWARD SKEMPTON

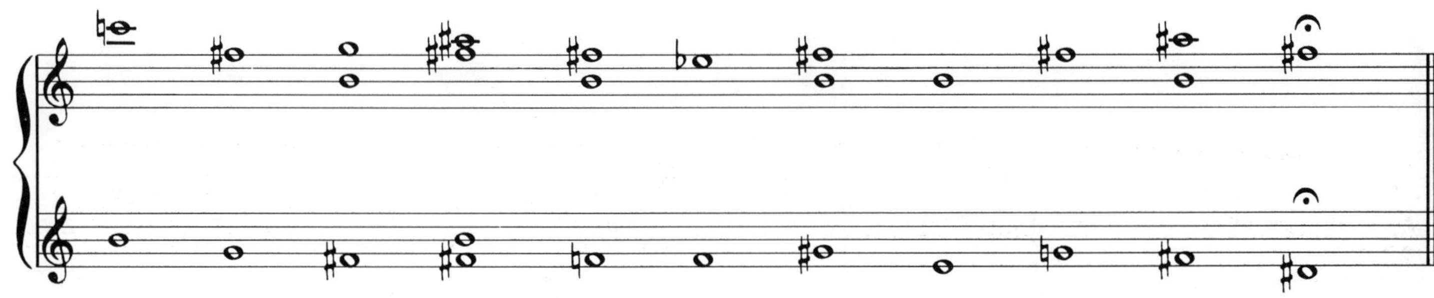

1 January 1981

for John Tilbury

Swedish Caprice

HOWARD SKEMPTON

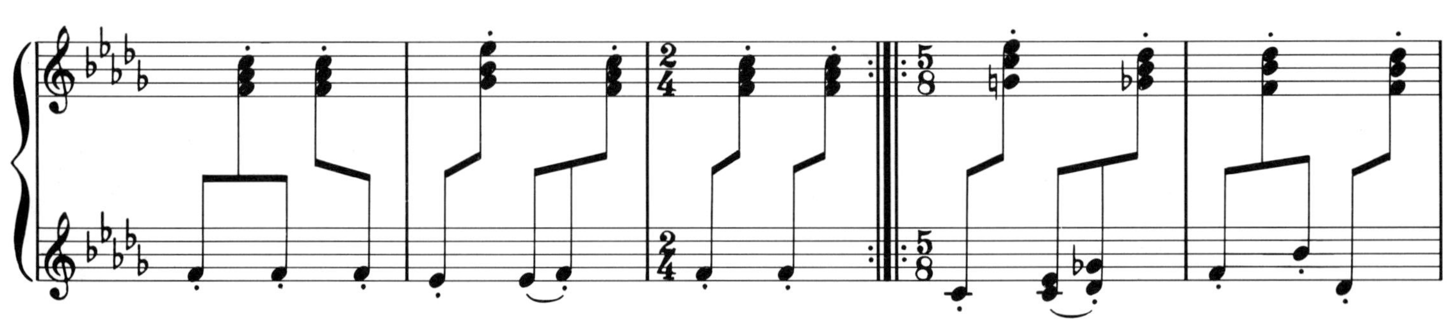

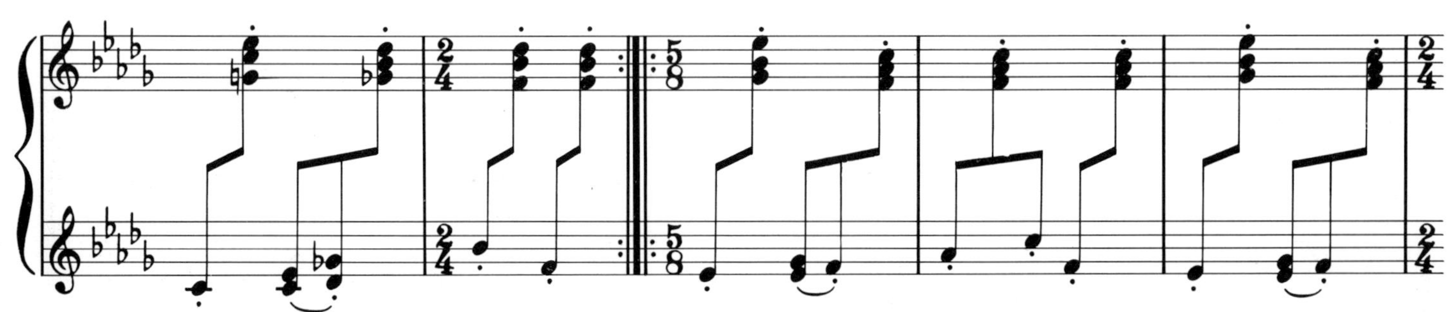

2 April 1993

to Peter and Mollie du Sautoy

Quavers 3

HOWARD SKEMPTON

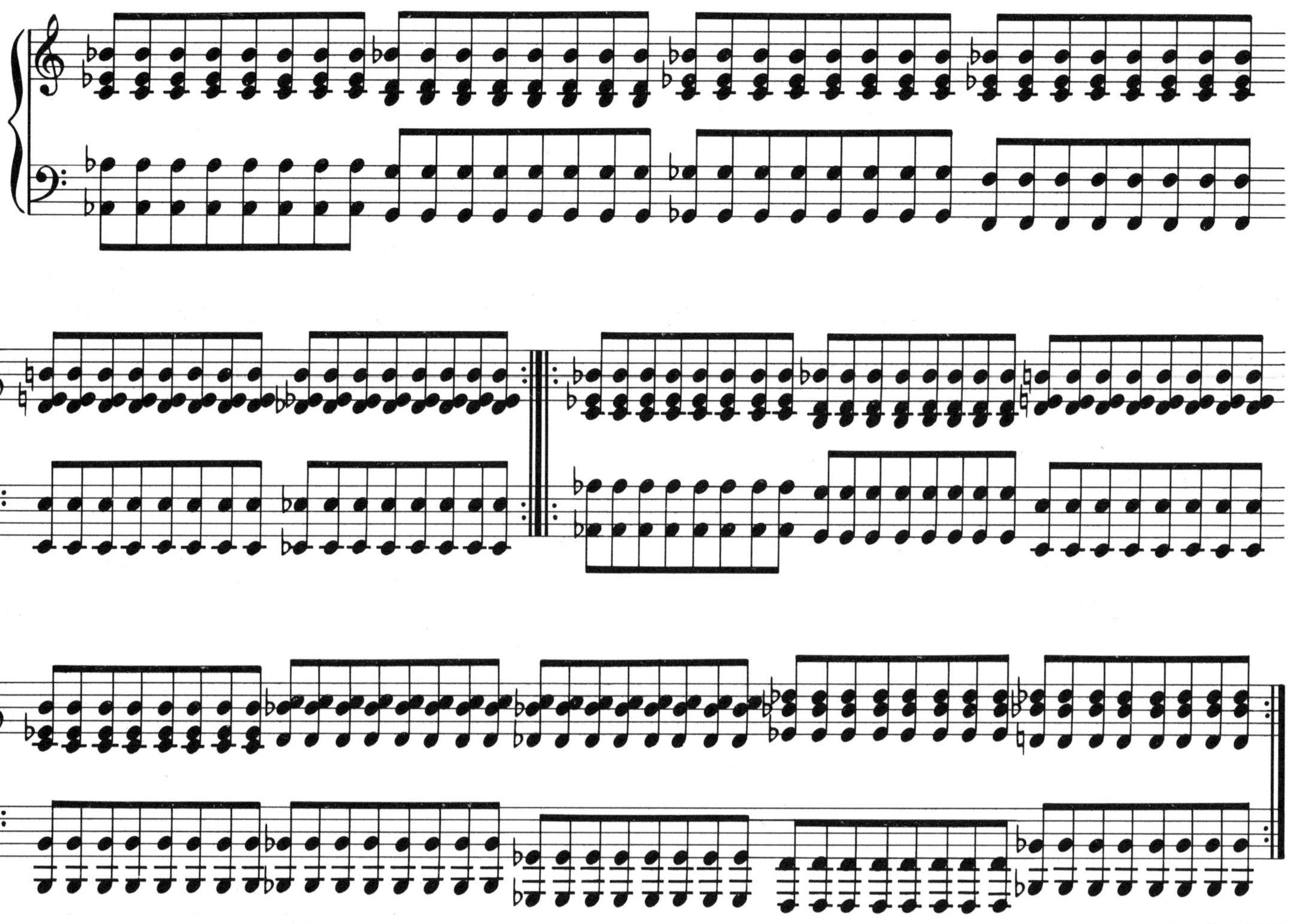

April 1975

for Dave Smith

una barcarola eccentrica

HOWARD SKEMPTON

August 1989

for John Tilbury

The Durham Strike

HOWARD SKEMPTON

Slowly

pp

Ped.

(Ped.)

(pedalling free to the end)

smorz.
Extremely slowly
January 1985

Postlude

HOWARD SKEMPTON

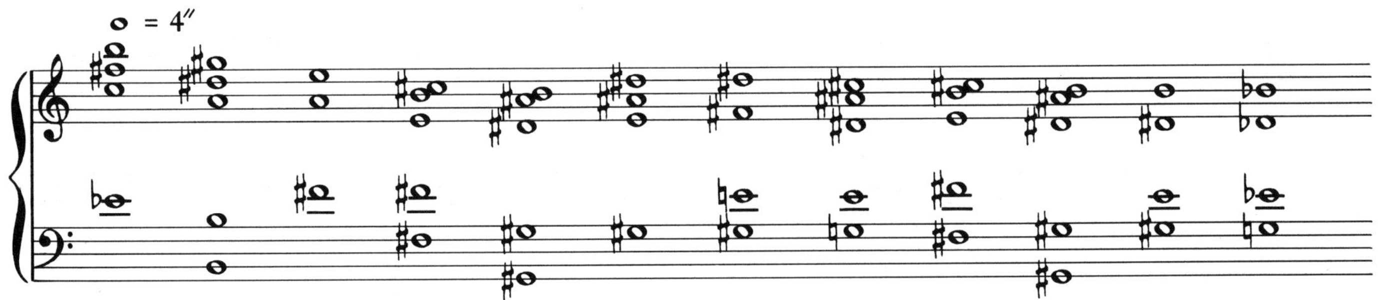

12 November 1978

to my niece Kyra, born 13 July 1979, and my nephews, Simon and Daniel

Friday's Child

HOWARD SKEMPTON

𝅗𝅥 = 2″

p

13 July 1979

for John McAlpine

Resolution

HOWARD SKEMPTON

December 1986

for John Tilbury

Two Highland Dances

HOWARD SKEMPTON

No. 1. Play 4 times, not too slowly

July 1970

No. 2. Play 4 times ♩ = less than 60

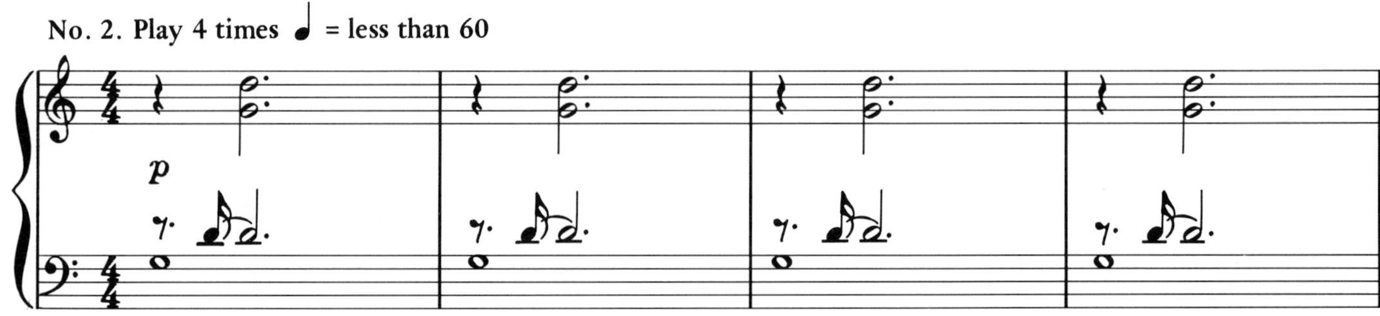

In both pieces, use sustaining pedal to sustain through rests.

July 1970

for Sally

Memento

HOWARD SKEMPTON

Slowly and quietly

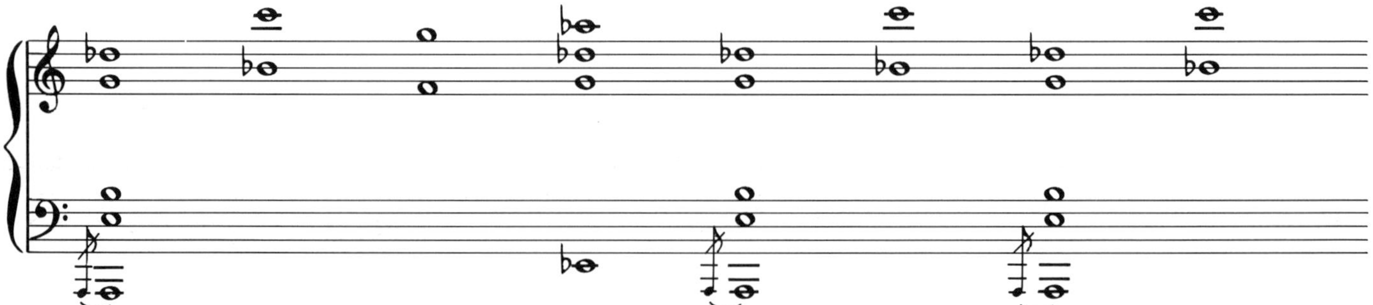

13 December 1978

for Donald and Kathleen Mitchell

Tender Melody

HOWARD SKEMPTON

15 November 1974

One for Martha

HOWARD SKEMPTON

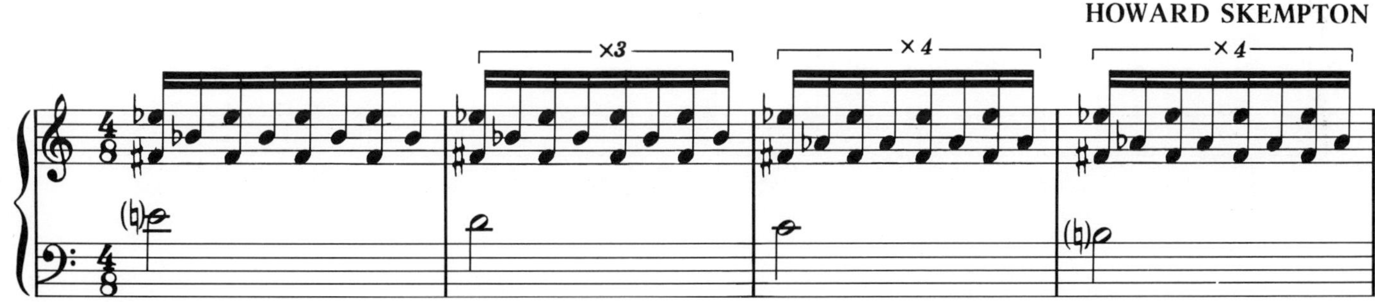

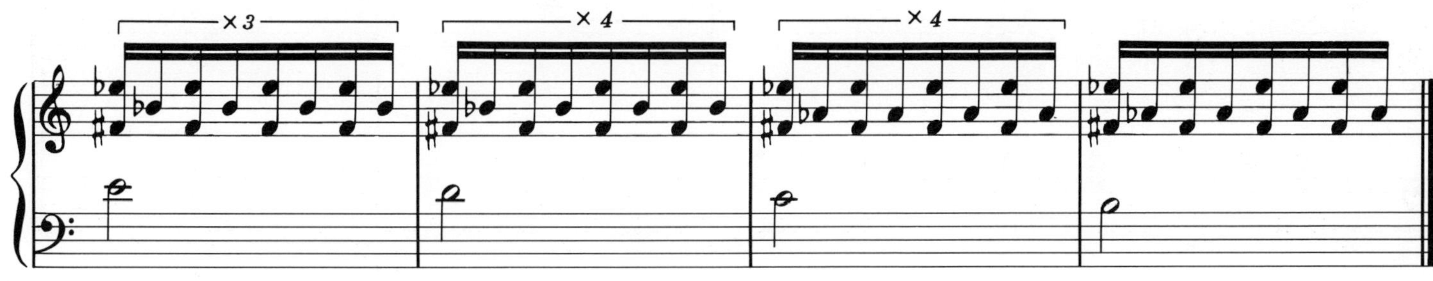

May 1974

Sweet Chariot

HOWARD SKEMPTON

April 1973

Piano Piece for Trevor Clarke

HOWARD SKEMPTON

August 1985

Quavers 2

HOWARD SKEMPTON

27 July 1974

for Donald on his birthday

Second Gentle Melody

HOWARD SKEMPTON

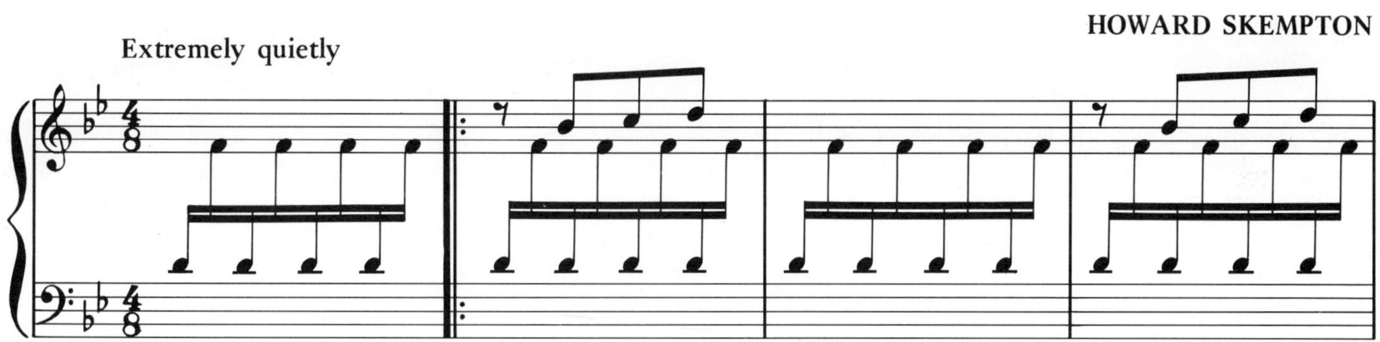

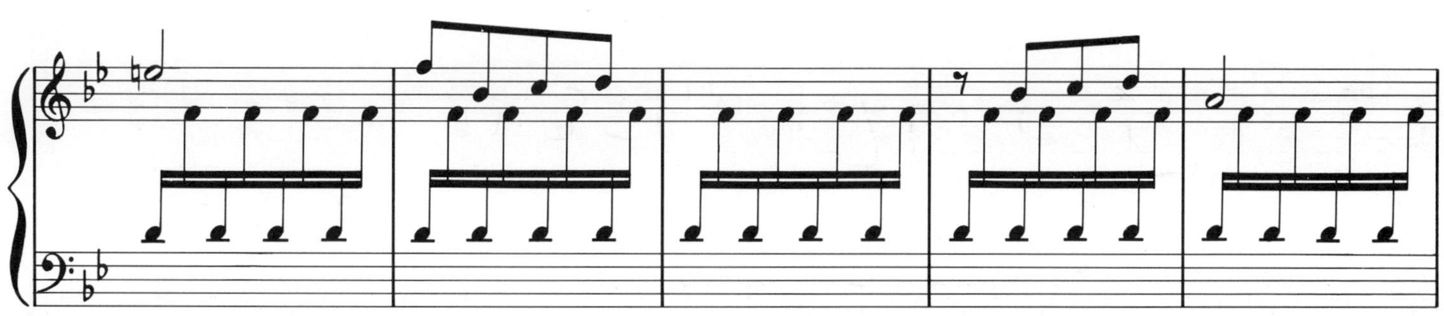

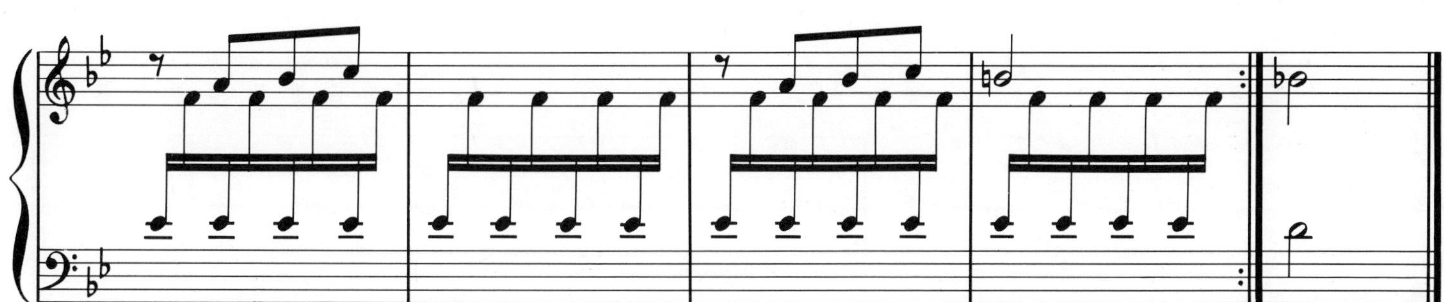

6 February 1975

Colonnade

HOWARD SKEMPTON

Very slowly and quietly

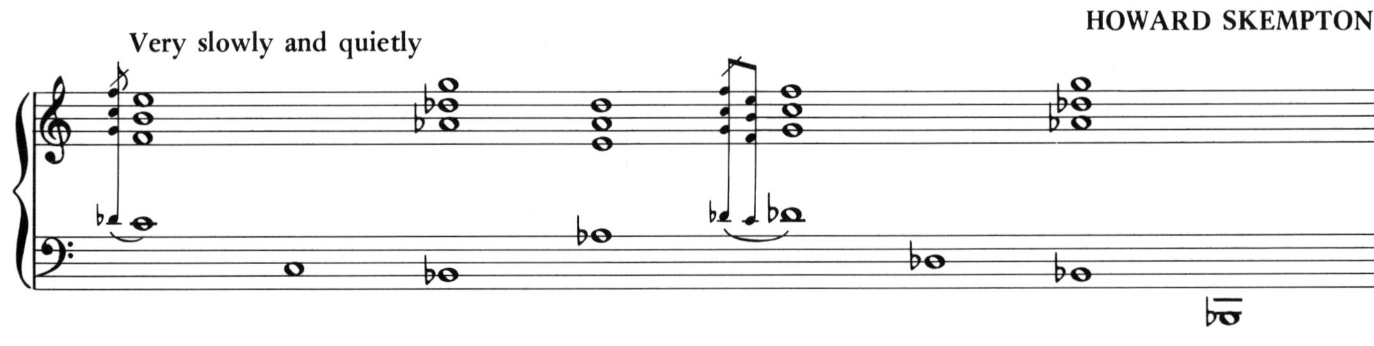

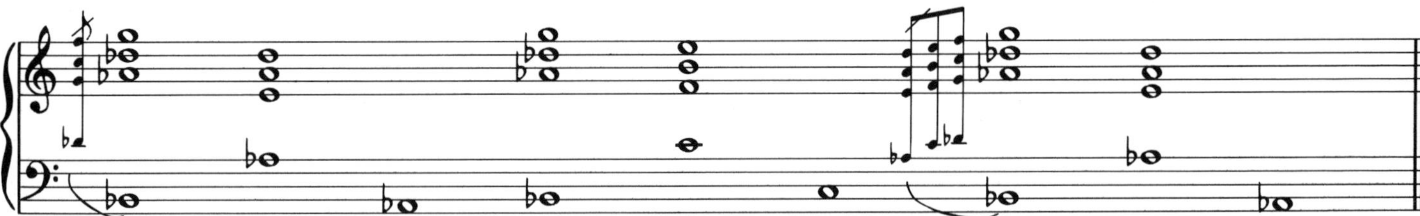

Accidentals apply only to the notes they immediately precede.

17 February 1975

for Dreamtiger

Surface Tension 3

HOWARD SKEMPTON

Gently

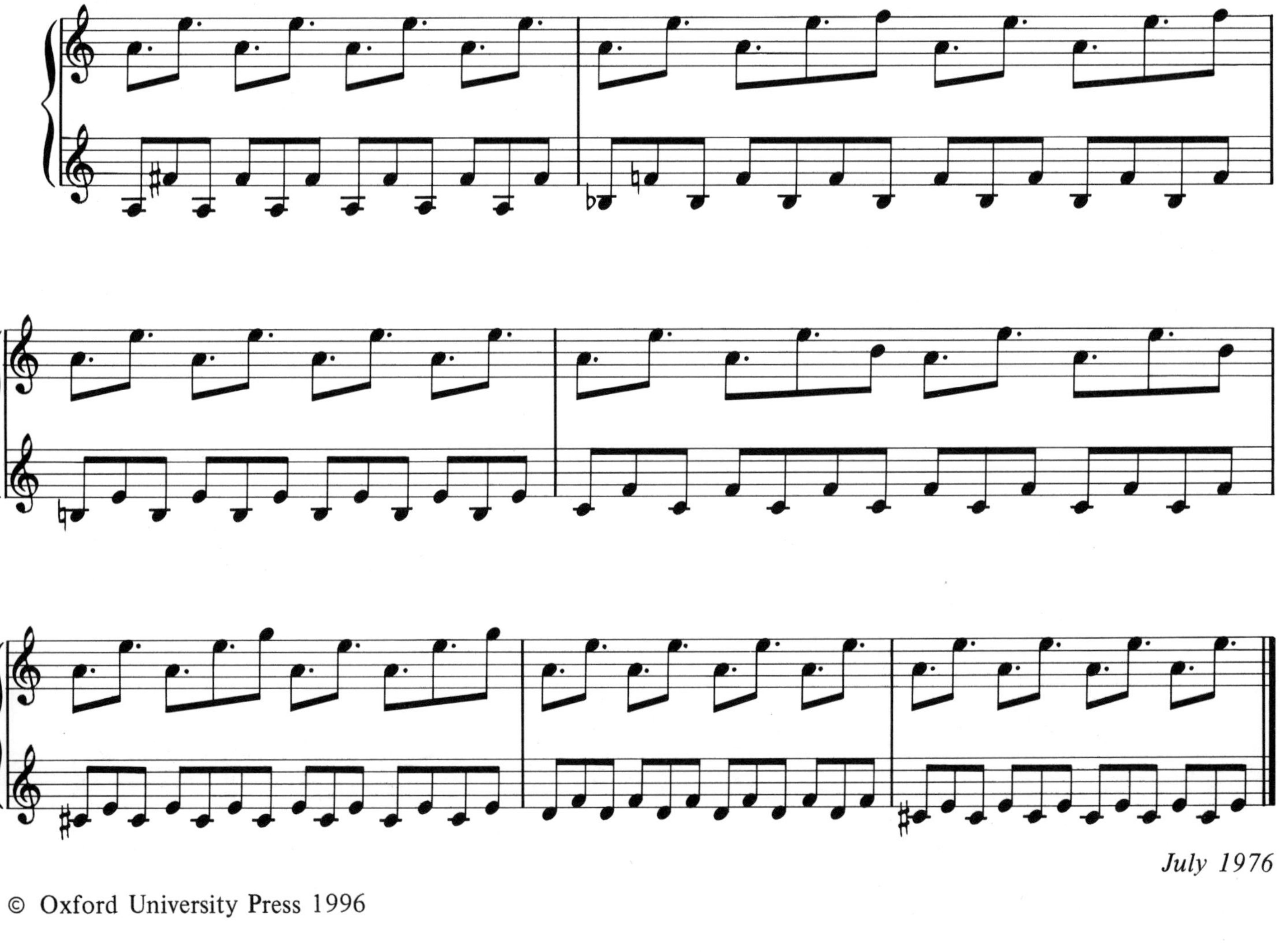

July 1976

to Imogen

Seascape

HOWARD SKEMPTON

Gently

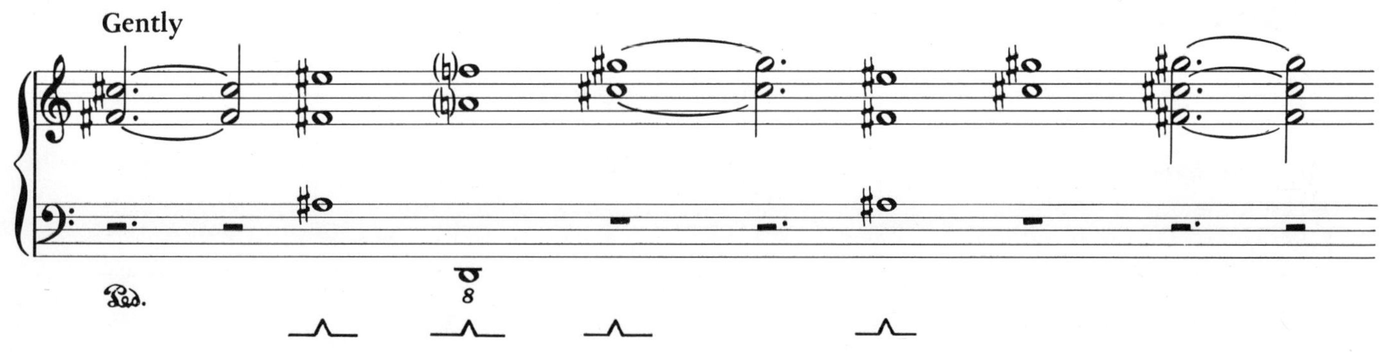

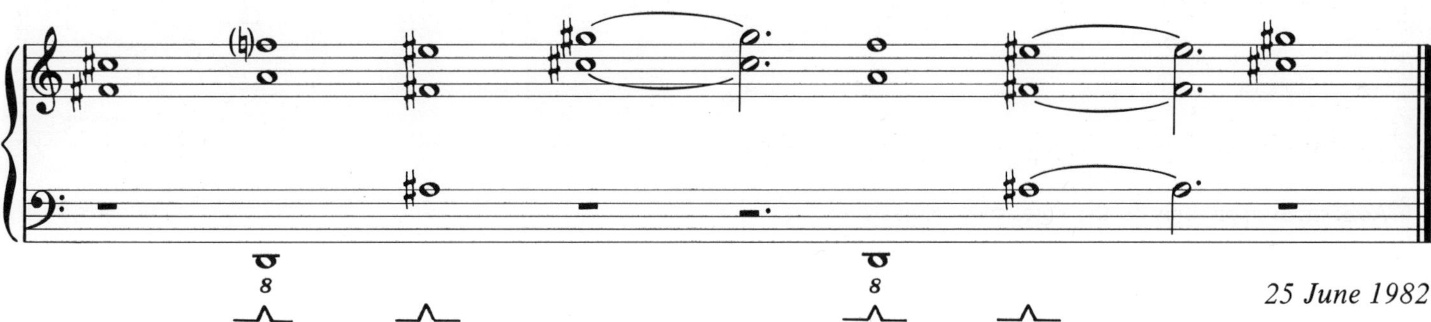

25 June 1982

Beginner

HOWARD SKEMPTON

Gently

19 April 1983

for Giancarlo Cardini

Campanella 4

HOWARD SKEMPTON

August 1985

for John Tilbury

The Mold Riots

HOWARD SKEMPTON

II
♪ = c. 112
brightly
brightly
mp delicately
f
mp delicately
f
ff massively
mp
(mp)
f
mp
f
ff
mp
mf

brightly
brightly
mp delicately
f
mp delicately
f
ff massively
mp
to Michael Finnissy
after - image
HOWARD SKEMPTON
Ped.
14 March 1990

to John Tilbury

Maestoso

HOWARD SKEMPTON

April 1990

to Justin Connolly

Ring in the Valiant

HOWARD SKEMPTON

March 1993

Printed and bound in Great Britain by
Caligraving Limited Thetford Norfolk